DATE DUE			
DEC 30 1992			
DEC 13 1993			
DEC 30 1993			
FEB 24 1994			
AUG 17 1994			
OCT 22 1994			
NOV 26 1994			
JAN 3 1995			
DEC 16 1996			

A CHRISTMAS CELEBRATION

TRADITIONS AND CUSTOMS FROM AROUND THE WORLD

WRITTEN BY
PAMELA KENNEDY

ART RESEARCH BY
F. LYNNE BACHLEDA

IDEALS CHILDREN'S BOOKS • NASHVILLE, TENNESSEE

For Douglas, who fills each day with Christmas joy.

- P.K.

Text copyright © 1992 by Pamela Kennedy
Illustrations copyright © 1992 by Ideals Publishing Corporation

Published by Ideals Publishing Corporation
Nashville, Tennessee 37214

Printed and bound in Mexico.

Library of Congress Cataloging-in-Publication Data

Kennedy, Pamela.
    A Christmas celebration: traditions and customs from around the world/written by Pamela Kennedy; art research by F. Lynne Bachleda.
        p.   cm.
    Includes index.
    Summary: Explains the customs and traditions of Christmas, including those of pre-Christian origin, and discusses how the holiday is celebrated around the world.
    ISBN 0-8249-8587-7 (lib. bdg.)—ISBN 0-8249-8551-6 (trade)
    1. Christmas—Juvenile literature. [1. Christmas.]
I. Bachleda, F. Lynne. II. Title.
GT4985.5.K46   1992
394.2'68282—dc20   92-6135
                                           CIP
                                           AC

The display type is Shelley Allegro.
The text type is Berkeley.
Color separations made by Chapter One.

Art credits:

Front cover *Nativity*. Elim Lutheran Church, Robbinsdale, Minnesota. The Crosiers/Gene Plaisted. **Back cover** *Madonna with Baby*, Botticelli. Scala/Art Resource, NY. **3** *Madonna Tempi*, Raffaello. Scala/Art Resource, NY. **4** *Vierge de Lorette*, Raphael. Lauros-Giraudon/Art Resource, NY. **5** *Epiphany*, Fra Angelico. SuperStock. **6-7** *Cutting Mistletoe*. North Wind Picture Archives. **8-9** *Reform of the Calendar,* Travoletta di Bicerna. Scala/Art Resource, NY. **10** *Christmas Candlelight*. Ideals Photo Archives. **11** *Hauling in the Yule Log,* H.M. Paget. North Wind Picture Archives. **12** *Magi*. Nativity Church, St. Paul, Minnesota. The Crosiers/Gene Plaisted. **13** *Nativity Shepherds*. St. Paul's United Methodist Church, Lincoln, Nebraska. The Crosiers/Gene Plaisted. **14** (top) *Cutting the Christmas Tree*. North Wind Picture Archives. (bottom) *Christmas Tree*. Morning Star. **15** (top) *Happy Carolers*. Ideals Photo Archives. (bottom) *Trimming the Tree*. North Wind Picture Archives. **16** *Under the Mistletoe*. North Wind Picture Archives. **17** (top) *Sprig of Mistletoe*, Mauritius-Hubatka. The Photo Source. (bottom) *Poinsettia*. SuperStock. **18** *A Nativity Scene*. H. Armstrong Roberts. **19** *In the Stable*. Zefa/H. Armstrong Roberts. **20** (top) *Gift for the Little One*. North Wind Picture Archives. (bottom) *A Christmas Card*. Superstock. **21** (top) *Boxing Day*. North Wind Picture Archives. (bottom) *Underneath the Christmas Tree*. Ideals Photo Archives. **22** *Plum Pudding*. The Anthony Blake Photo Library. **23** *Christmas Sweets*. The Anthony Blake Photo Library. **24** (top) *Angel Announcing the Birth of Christ to the Shepherds*, Robert Leinweber. Superstock. (bottom) *Little Carolers*. North Wind Picture Archives. **25** *Carols*. North Wind Picture Archives. **26** *Saint Nicholas*. Superstock. **27** *Saint Nicholas*. Holy Cross, Liege, Belgium. The Crosiers/Gene Plaisted. **28** (top) *An Advent Wreath*. Superstock. (bottom) *Christmas Eve*. North Wind Picture Archives. **29** *Nativity*. Trinity Lutheran Church, Rochester, Minnesota. The Crosiers/Gene Plaisted. **30** *Les Roses de Thory*, P.J. Redoute. Giraudon/Art Resource.

ONTENTS

*I*n those days Caesar Augustus issued a decree that a census should be taken of the entire Roman world. . . . And everyone went to his own town to register. So Joseph also went up . . . to Bethlehem the town of David, because he belonged to the house and line of David. He went there to register with Mary, who was pledged to be married to him and was expecting a child. While they were there, the time came for the baby to be born, and she gave birth to her firstborn, a son. She wrapped him in cloths and placed him in a manger, because there was no room for them in the inn.

Luke 2:1, 3-7

The story of the very first Christmas is as simple and touching today as it was two thousand years ago. Since that holy night, Christmas has become the most festive Christian holiday, embracing a whole season of celebration.

The Christmas season stretches for weeks and includes special days like St. Lucia's Day and Epiphany, important symbols like stars and candles, and delightful customs like gift-giving and feasting.

Many of the customs enjoyed at Christmastime began long before the birth of Jesus. As people from all over the world accepted Christianity, however, they gave their ancient customs new meanings connected to their faith in Christ.

*M*idwinter was a time of great superstition in ancient communities. At the time of the winter solstice, when the earth's equator is farthest from the sun and the days are their shortest, people often grew fearful. They thought the sun had become weak and might not have enough strength to return in the spring. If this happened, their crops and animals would die. These prehistoric people hoped that by holding festivals and celebrations to honor the sun, they could encourage it to return and shine brightly once more.

In ancient Rome, people held Saturnalia, a week-long festival honoring their god of agriculture, Saturn, whose symbol was the sun. During this celebration from December 17-23, business stopped, military exercises ceased, and school classes dismissed.

Saturnalia was a time of goodwill when people visited friends and relatives, exchanged gifts, and held feasts. Homes were decorated with evergreens and candles. Slaves and masters exchanged places for the holiday, and everyone tried to forget grudges and forgive one another.

In ancient Persia, which is modern-day Iran, the winter solstice was a time for lighting candles and fires to honor their god of light, Mithra. Followers of Mithra, called Zoastrians, believed that their god had been born on December 25, and on that day, they held feasts and celebrations to honor Mithra's birthday.

*I*n the cold, dark winters of Scandinavia, the Vikings lit huge bonfires and held yuletide, a two-week-long festival in honor of their god Thor. Viking families brought evergreen boughs into their homes and invited guests to share special meals. Yuletide was held in January, and during the celebration, all regular work came to a halt, and everyone was encouraged to mend quarrels with neighbors, perform kind deeds, and gather with family and friends.

Long ago in North America, members of the Iroquois tribes held their midwinter ceremonial for seven days. On the first day, the ashes of their longhouse fires were stirred to symbolize the scattering of the old year fire and the lighting of the new. On the days following, there would be feasting, storytelling, dancing, and games.

Besides the fires, gifts, and feasts of the ancient festivals, a spirit of joy and goodwill filled people's hearts. Old battles were forgotten, and during the time of the celebration, even enemies tried to get along.

The first Christians were forbidden by the Roman government to practice their faith, so they worshiped secretly in caves called the Catacombs. On the Catacomb walls beneath Rome are ancient drawings of the Magi worshiping the infant Jesus, which indicates that early Christians celebrated Jesus' birth—but there are no records of when this occurred. Even the Bible does not record Jesus' date of birth.

During the first few centuries after Jesus' death, the early church was established, but many different dates were used to celebrate his birthday. In A.D. 320, Pope Julius I and other Roman church leaders agreed on December 25 as the official date of Christ's birth. This date was chosen for several reasons.

Many early believers had adopted March 25 as the time when the angel told Mary she would bear the holy child—nine months from this date was December 25. In addition, December 25 corresponded to many non-Christian winter festivals, and it was also celebrated as the birthday of the Persian sun god, Mithra. By placing Christmas on this date, church founders hoped to make it easier for new believers to turn from worship of the sun to belief in the Son of God, Jesus.

Today, December 25 is celebrated as Christ's birthday in most Christian churches. There are some, however, such as both the Greek Orthodox and the Russian Orthodox churches, in which January 6 is the preferred date.

The very first Christians celebrated Christ's birthday as the "Feast of the Nativity." But by the time of the Roman Emperor Constantine in the third century, it was also called Christmas—a word made from combining the name of Christ with the word mass, meaning celebration or rite. The word, Christmas, therefore, means the celebration of Christ and is the name for this holiday in most English-speaking countries.

Noel or Nowell is another word used to describe Christmas. This word comes from shortening the French phrase *le bonnes nouvelles,* which means "the good news of the Gospel." The Christmas season in France is called *la fête de Noel.*

In Spain and Italy, *Il Natale* is the common term for Christmas. It means "the birthday." *Yule, Jul,* or *Ule* is the name given to the Christmas season in Scotland and Scandinavian countries. This title has its roots in ancient celebrations honoring the sun.

The German name for Christmastime is *das Christfest* or *Weihnachten.* In Portugal, it is *O Natal.* The Greek call it *Khristougenna,* and in Holland, it is *Kerstrnis. Rozhdestvo* is the name for Christmas in Russia, the Rumanian word is *Cracrunul,* and the Polish call it *Boze Narodzenie.*

*F*irelight and evergreens and feasting and gift-giving were all a part of midwinter festivities long before Jesus was born. As Christianity spread across the continents, new believers gave the old customs new meaning connected with the birth of Christ.

From prehistoric times, people have wondered at the almost magical beauty of fire. Ancient people thought that all fire came from the sun, and they honored it with candles, torches, and bonfires.

As Christians began to celebrate the birth of Jesus, they recalled his words, "I am the light of the world." The candle flame reminded them of this, so people began to use candles in Christmas celebrations.

Hundreds of years ago, during the Middle Ages, Christians told legends about the Christ child traveling through the night looking for a place to stay. On Christmas Eve, families placed lighted candles in their windows as a welcome sign to the little wanderer. On that night, no stranger was turned away from the door.

Since then, the custom of placing candles in the windows at Christmastime is continued in many homes. Some families frame their doors and windows with colored lights, offering a bright greeting to all who come for a Christmas visit.

In the cold, dark winters of the northern countries, the shortest day of the year, December 21, was a day of great celebration. The Norsemen rejoiced that the days would begin to lengthen and the sun's light would return to warm the earth. To celebrate the return of light and heat, the people burned huge logs on December 21. They thought of the sun as a wheel of fire rolling toward and away from the earth as the seasons changed, and the enormous pieces of wood were called yule logs from the Norse word for wheel: *hweol*.

While people in northern Europe no longer worship the sun, the yule log, or Christmas log, is often a part of their holiday celebrations. Lit on Christmas Eve as the family gathers, the yule log burns through the night. A piece of the old log is sometimes saved to use when lighting a new log the following year. Although many modern homes no longer have fireplaces, the yule log remains a Christmas symbol— often as a log-shaped cake or ice cream dessert.

*W*hen Jesus was born, there were wise men called Magi who studied the movements of the planets and heavenly constellations. When an especially bright star appeared in the sky, they left their homes to find its meaning, traveling across deserts and mountains.

> *. . . they went their way and the star they had seen in the east went ahead of them until it stopped over the place where the child was. When they saw the star they were overjoyed.* Matthew 2:9-10

For centuries, people have wondered about that star. Today, scientists know it could not have been a comet or a meteor that guided these men because their trip lasted a long time. It has been discovered, however, that there was an unusual occurrence in the heavens at the time of Christ's birth. The planets of Mars, Jupiter, and Saturn appeared together, forming a brilliant grouping called Pisces. Some people think this was the star of Bethlehem, while others believe there was a miraculous appearance of a special new star just at that time.

Today, children in many countries watch the evening sky on Christmas Eve for the first star to appear as a signal to begin their Christmas celebrations. Others walk from house to house on Three Kings Eve, January 5, led by a child who carries a star high on a pole. They pretend they are the wise men searching for baby Jesus. At each home they pass, they stop and sing and are offered treats as a reward.

*A*ngels brought the message of Jesus' birth long ago, and since then, angels have become a symbol of peace on earth. Peace was especially welcomed by the poor shepherds who lived in a land occupied by the Roman army, but throughout history, people all over the world have longed for peace.

Ancient winter festivals of the Norsemen pre-dating Christ focused on this longing as warring groups declared a Peacestead, or season of peace, during the darkest weeks of winter. During the Roman Saturnalia, war was outlawed and civil disputes were settled.

Today, our Christmas seasons are often marked by reflections of the angels' message of peace on earth as Christmas cease-fires and the release of political prisoners are arranged during the holiday period.

In many countries, the angels' declaration of peace is an important part of the Christmas celebration. During Christmas church services in Lebanon, Christians repeat the angels' words, then each touches the hand of the person to his or her right. This tradition of "the touch of peace" is called a *salaam*. Polish and Ukrainian believers eat a small peace wafer before their Christmas feast. It reminds the family members of the Christmas message brought by angels so long ago.

In North America, angels often top Christmas trees, while in South America, they stand with outstretched wings over a manger scene. Wherever they appear at Christmastime, angels symbolize the message of love and peace that is central to the holiday.

*A*s with many other symbols of Christmas, the Christmas tree had its beginnings long before the time of Christ. Many cultures, such as ancient Greeks and Romans, trace their beginnings to a legend involving trees. Middle Eastern cultures trace their roots to a world tree, and the Chinese tell ancient stories of a sacred willow.

Ancient Celtic tribes, who lived throughout western Europe until 100 B.C., selected the tallest, most beautiful tree in their settlement as a "mother tree." Left standing in the center of a community, the mother tree served as a meeting place for all business and ceremonies.

Although trees in general were very important to early people, the evergreen tree was especially honored. When all other plants dropped their leaves and stood bare and stark in winter, the rich green firs and pines reminded people that life would continue. For this reason, the evergreen became a central symbol in many midwinter festivals.

In ancient Rome, people decorated evergreens with small candles and figures representing their sun god during Saturnalia and used the fragrant boughs to decorate their homes. The ancient Celtic Druids in France, Great Britain, and Ireland decorated their sacred trees with candles and golden fruit during the winter solstice.

During the Middle Ages, the "paradise tree" was a central prop in religious plays performed by troupes of actors traveling through northern Europe. A fir tree was decorated with apples to represent the garden of Eden as the actors told the story of Adam and Eve. Since these plays were usually performed at Christmastime, the decorated paradise tree became associated with this holiday.

The custom of decorating an evergreen tree inside a house may be traced to Martin Luther, who was a German preacher. One Christmas Eve, it is said, Martin Luther walked in the woods near his home and saw the tall fir trees against the starry sky. He cut down a small fir, took it home, and decorated it with candles. Then he gathered his children around the twinkling tree and told them about the stars that shone above Bethlehem on the night Jesus was born.

Decorating indoor Christmas trees spread from Germany, through Europe, and to America. German immigrants to the United States originated the custom of hanging cookies and candles on their trees, while Swedish and Norwegian families added delicate ornaments of braided and woven straw. Early Americans used garlands of popcorn and cranberries, as well as figures fashioned from dry cornhusks.

MAKING A CHRISTMAS TREE FOR THE ANIMALS

string	peanut butter
1 pine cone	wild bird seed

During the winter months, birds and small animals have a hard time finding food to eat. As a holiday gift to these creatures, make a small Christmas tree. First, tie string around the small end of a pine cone. Keeping the string out of the way, spread peanut butter on the pine cone, then roll it in wild bird seed. Hang it outside on a nearby tree.

15

The evergreen is not the only Christmas plant traced to prehistoric wintertime festivals. Mistletoe and holly have longstanding histories, as well as meanings connected with Christianity.

Ancient Druids felt trees to be sacred, and they thought that mistletoe was magical. During their winter festivals, they cut it from the branches of an oak or apple tree with a curved, golden knife and caught it in white cloths before it could touch the ground. They believed that the green leaves and waxy, white berries brought love and good luck to those who hung sprigs of the plant in their homes.

The Druids also wore holly in their hair during their midwinter celebrations, and ancient Romans used holly in their Saturnalia festivals. As Christianity spread, early followers saw the evergreen leaves as a symbol of God's everlasting love, and they connected the red berries with the crucifixion.

Today, mistletoe and holly wreaths and swags decorate doorways and fireplaces. The shiny holly leaves and bright berries combine the traditional Christmas colors of green and red. And tradition says that if someone stands under the mistletoe, they must be kissed or will be unlucky in love during the coming year.

The poinsettia is the flower most symbolic of Christmas in the United States. In 1828, Dr. Joel Poinsett, a U.S. minister to Mexico, brought the plant known as the "Flower of the Holy Night" to his country. The red, star-shaped blossoms gained immediate popularity as a Christmas flower, and the plant was renamed to honor Poinsett. Perhaps much of the poinsettia's appeal comes from the beautiful Mexican legend that attempts to explain its origin.

THE LEGEND OF THE POINSETTIA

Long ago in Mexico, a little girl stood outside a church on Christmas Eve. She watched others taking gifts inside to place before a statue of baby Jesus. The longer she watched, the worse she felt because she had nothing to give. An angel saw the sad little girl and spoke to her.

"Gather the weeds beside the roadside and take them to the holy child," the angel said. Drying her tears, the little girl obeyed. She gathered a large armful of the green, leafy weeds and carried them inside. But as she walked up the aisle, the people laughed at her gift.

The embarrassed little girl placed her branches beside the manger, and suddenly a miracle occurred. The green leaves turned to brilliant red! Now every year at Christmastime, the green leaves of the poinsettia turn bright red to honor the Son of God born so long ago.

While the Christmas tree is the primary Christmas decoration in many places, in most southern European nations and in Central and South America, the Christmas crib or manger is the center of attention.

The custom of having a scene of the holy family, angels, shepherds, and even animals was begun by St. Francis of Assisi in 1224. He wanted everyone to be able to understand the events in the Bible and to better appreciate God's gift of His Son. In the city of Creccio, Italy, St. Francis built a stable. Then he dressed people as Mary, Joseph, and the shepherds. He brought in straw, cows, a donkey, and some sheep. Last of all, he placed a small, wax doll in the manger to represent baby Jesus. The townspeople enjoyed the living nativity scene so much that they decided to repeat it every Christmas.

Today, nativity scenes of wood, plastic, china, or plaster may be found in homes around the world. In France, it is called a *creche,* or cradle, and in Spain it is a *nacimiento,* or nativity scene. In Germany, a manger is a *krippe,* and in Italy, it is a *presepio.* The custom is often to leave the manger empty until Christmas Eve, when a figure of baby Jesus is placed inside.

In the countries of South America, children write notes to the Christ child and place them beside the manger in their *nacimiento.* They believe that if they are very good, the angels will deliver their notes to heaven so that Jesus may read them.

In Mexico, there is a favorite custom based on the nativity story called *Las Posadas,* a name which comes from the word meaning inn or lodging. Beginning on December 16, the custom of *Las Posadas* continues for nine evenings. Each night, townspeople reenact the holy family's search for a place to stay. Knocking on doors, they ask for lodging until they are finally given entrance to a home where everyone enjoys fireworks and a party feast. On Christmas Eve, the final and most impressive *Posada* takes place. The players carry an image of the Christ child and, at the end of the evening, place it in the crib in the *nacimiento.* The actors playing the parts of the holy family, shepherds, and angels kneel before the Christ child and offer prayers to God.

A Merry Christmas

efore the birth of Christ, people gave one another gifts during their wintertime festivals. In Rome, during Saturnalia, this custom was called *strenae*. At first, friends and relatives exchanged simple things like flowers and tree branches, but later, they added other gifts such as foods, candles, and small statues of their gods.

Giving gifts became connected with Jesus' birth when the Magi brought gold, frankincense, and myrrh to the Christ child. The earliest Christmas gifts were simple things such as sweets, fruits, and trinkets.

Today, friends and families may exchange elaborate gifts, but friendly greetings expressed in Christmas cards are reminders of a simpler time. The custom of sending cards to loved ones at Christmas began about 150 years ago. The first cards were hand drawn by an English artist named John Horsley in 1843. His design featured a smiling family gathered around a dinner table, and on either side of the family were scenes depicting acts of kindness.

Because printing and postage were expensive until the late 1800s, the sending of Christmas cards was limited prior to that time. With the introduction of cheaper and faster printing methods and the half-cent stamp in 1870, sending Christmas cards became a popular custom. Today, over two billion Christmas cards pass through the world's post offices each year.

*B*esides giving gifts and sending cards to friends and family, giving food and other gifts to needy strangers has long been a custom of Christmas. This is a reflection of thanks for God's gift of His son Jesus to the world.

Long ago in England, the day after Christmas was set aside for acts of charity. On this date, called Boxing Day, boxes of food and clothing are given to those less fortunate. In many parts of Spain, January 5, or Epiphany Eve, is the time when gifts are collected and distributed to the poor. Christians in Syria prepare special gifts for the poor on December 3, St. Barbara's Eve. Syrian children deliver the gifts of food so that they may practice being thoughtful and unselfish.

In the United States, community and church groups volunteer to prepare Christmas dinners for the less fortunate. Schools collect warm clothing and toys to give to homeless children. And some churches hold "White Christmas" services where members bring donations of food for the needy wrapped in white tissue paper. Giving to those who have nothing to give in return reflects the true spirit of Christmas.

*L*ong before Christianity, wintertime festivals featured many of the same foods popular to Christmas feasts today. In the ancient lands which are now England, Ireland, Scandinavia, and even Yugoslavia, the main dish at a winter festival was the wild boar. Today, in many of the countries of central and northern Europe, the eating of a Christmas ham or pork roast is traced to this ancient custom.

Other Christmas foods are traced to ancient winter festivals. During the Saturnalia in Rome, cooks prepared special sweets to be given to friends as gifts. People in the Ukraine baked breads and cakes in honor of the gods of the fields and hoped that these offerings might cause the gods to bless them with good crops the following year.

During the Middle Ages, Christmas pies became a popular main course in England and are even recalled in the favorite nursery rhyme *Little Jack Horner.* Another favorite English dish was plum pudding. It actually contained no plums, but was made of suet, flour, sugar, raisins, nuts, and spices. These ingredients were mixed together, tied loosely in a cloth, and cooked in a pot of boiling water. As it boiled, the ingredients enlarged to fill the cloth, becoming "plum," or just right. When finished, it was unwrapped, sliced like a heavy cake, topped with cream, and served at the end of the Christmas meal.

Most American Christmas foods have their origins in Europe. An exception, however, is the cranberry. Near the Plymouth settlement of the Pilgrims, the Native Americans introduced their new neighbors to the tart, red berry growing in nearby bogs. Since then, cranberry sauces have become a traditional part of American holiday menus.

Cookies, cakes, and other sweets are still favorite Christmas treats. Each country seems to have its specialty. The French make delicious rolled cakes called yule logs, while German cooks bake *pfeffernuesse,* or gingerbread cookies, cut into holiday shapes. Scotland is famous for buttery shortbread, and from Sweden come yeast buns called *Lussekake,* honoring St. Lucia. Breads made with candied fruit and raisins are favorites in Denmark, Switzerland, and Italy.

In all countries where Christmas is celebrated, people gather to share special meals. Even the smallest of gatherings becomes a festive time for food and fun.

RECIPE FOR FROSTED FRUIT SWEETMEATS

2 egg whites	½ cup white, granulated sugar
1 T. water	assorted fruits and berries

In a small bowl, mix egg whites and water with a fork or whisk until frothy, but not stiff. Wash and dry individual pieces of fruit, such as grapes, cherries, and berries and set aside. Place sugar in a separate small bowl. Dip small bunches of grapes or individual pieces of fruit into egg white mixture, then place the fruit in the sugar, rolling to coat. Shake off extra sugar and place fruit on a wire rack to dry. These may be eaten alone or used to decorate other Christmas dishes.

The very first Christmas carol was not from earth, but sung by a choir of angels from heaven to a group of frightened shepherds.

Suddenly a great company of the heavenly host appeared with the angel praising God and saying, 'Glory to God in the highest, and on earth peace to men on whom his favor rests.' Luke 2:13-14

Many Christmas carols use passages from the Bible to relate the events surrounding the birth of Jesus. Early English carols also included Christmas symbols such as holly, ivy, and even a boar's head.

Caroling, or strolling from door to door singing the songs of Christmas, began in England long ago. Wandering musicians traveled from town to town visiting the castles of noblemen. They played and sang, hoping to receive a warm meal or coins for their efforts.

In warm climates, outdoor games were long associated with midwinter festivals. During ancient Roman Saturnalia, dances and parades were popular. But where winters were cold, it was difficult to go outside. People used their imaginations to help pass the time.

Long ago, Native Americans spent their cold winter hours listening to the "teller of tales" recount the myths of their tribes. During the Middle Ages in Europe, Christmas festivities often featured performances by storytellers, jugglers, poets, and singers.

In English-speaking countries, wintertime games were played in the family's sitting room, or parlor, and they became known as parlor games. One of the oldest of these associated with Christmas is Blind Man's Buff. Someone is blindfolded and tries to catch and identify another player—everyone calls out at once, trying to distract his or her attention. Whoever is caught first becomes the next "blind man."

Other old Christmas games include riddle asking, guessing games, coin tossing, and playing hide-and-seek. Singing and dancing were also popular Christmas activities, and many people thought these would help settle their stomachs after a huge Christmas dinner.

In Mexico, the breaking of a treat-filled piñata is a favorite Christmas game. Blindfolded children hit the paper-maché figure with sticks until it breaks; then they hurry to collect as much as possible.

HEUREUX NOËL

*M*ost children in the United States know about Santa Claus, but many do not realize that Saint Nicholas was a real person who lived over 1,700 years ago near modern-day Greece.

Nicholas traveled the countryside, helping poor people, praying for the sick, and encouraging little children. Well-known for his generosity, he gave almost all of his inherited wealth away. As stories of St. Nicholas spread, people began to give him credit whenever an unexpected gift came to them.

In the United States and England, children hang their stockings by the fireplace or on a bedpost on Christmas Eve. In Scandinavia, children set their shoes out on the hearth on Christmas Eve. These customs can be traced to old legends about Saint Nicholas.

According to the stories, there once were three poor sisters who could not marry because they had no money for a dowry. In order to help the girls, Nicholas tossed three small bags of gold into their home.

One legend records that the gold went down the chimney, and it landed in the girls' shoes on the hearth. Another version says that the gold flew in through an open window, and the bags landed in the girls' stockings, which were hung by the fire to dry. When the girls awoke in the morning, they found enough money to provide their dowries!

Nicholas died December 6 in A.D. 343, and in some parts of the world, people celebrate this as Saint Nicholas Day and exchange gifts.

The American version of Santa Claus in a fur-trimmed, red suit and riding in a sleigh pulled by flying reindeer is much newer than St. Nicholas. This image of Santa Claus comes from a nineteenth century poem, by Clement C. Moore, entitled *"The Night before Christmas."*

In Germany and Switzerland, it is *Christkind,* the Christ child, who brings gifts to good children, and St. Nicholas comes with him. In Czechoslovakia, children are told that St. Nicholas comes down from heaven on December 6, accompanied by an angel bearing gifts.

In some Scandinavian countries, the jolly elf *Jultomten* delivers gifts, driving a sleigh drawn by goats. English children wait for Father Christmas to fill their stockings, while French youngsters look for *Pere Noel* to place gifts in their empty shoes. On January 6, or Three Kings Day, Latin American children are given presents by the Magi.

Russian children wait for *Baboushka* during the night of January 5. Legends say that this elderly woman purposely gave the wise men the wrong directions to Bethlehem. She was sorry later and decided to take gifts to Jesus, but by then, she did not know where to find him. So each Christmas season, she leaves gifts on every child's bedside just in case that little one is Christ. In Italy, another lady known as *La Befana* does the same thing.

The traditions of gift givers who especially love children are almost as ancient as Christmas itself. Each of these characters reflects the spirit of love and sharing celebrated at this time of year.

The four weeks before Christmas Day are called Advent, which means arrival, in honor of Jesus' coming to earth.

An Advent tradition is to place a wreath of greenery and four candles on a table. Each Sunday before Christmas, one candle is lit and part of the Christmas story is told. On Christmas Eve, all four candles are lit, and often a fifth candle is lit in the center.

Early in the Advent season is St. Nicholas Eve, December 5, when children in Holland, France, and some areas of America leave empty shoes, food for the reindeer, and a note for St. Nicholas on their hearths.

The beginning of the Christmas season in Scandinavian counties is marked by St. Lucia's Day, on December 13. Early in the morning, the oldest daughter in each family dresses in a long, white gown. She wears an evergreen wreath with seven lighted candles on her head and serves her family breakfast in bed. This custom comes from the story of a brave young woman named Lucia who lived when Christians hid in caves to avoid capture—Lucia risked her life by taking food to the Christians, wearing candles on her head to light the dark caves.

Christmas Eve is a time for family gatherings and church services. Many families exchange gifts, while others hang up stockings to await the arrival of a gift-giver during the night. Christmas Eve is the time for lighting the yule log in many European homes—singing and dancing often accompany the hauling in of the huge, decorated log.

28

Few children must be coaxed out of bed on Christmas Day. Families travel to be with loved ones on this day, and special feasts are prepared. Church services are held, and the joyful songs of Christmas are sung by choirs.

In warm New Zealand and Australia, many families prepare roast turkey and go to the beach for a picnic. In the Ukraine, a traditional twelve-course meal is prepared on Christmas Day. A child watches at the window for the first evening star, the signal for the feast to begin.

The traditional "twelve days of Christmas" are the days from Christmas Day to Epiphany, or Twelfth Night, on January 6. Tradition says that three kings traveled from far away to visit the infant Jesus and arrived to see him on January 6. Another name for this date is Three Kings' Day.

January 6 is celebrated in addition to Christmas Day in Spain, France, and many Latin American countries, accompanied by gift-giving, feasting, and church services. Throughout the world, members of the Greek Orthodox church and the Russian Orthodox church honor January 6 as Christmas Day.

No matter which day is celebrated as Christ's birthday, the symbols and stories of this festive season combine in a tapestry of color and sound. Candles and carols, trees and stars, all remind us of the holy night long ago when God shared with the earth His Son and the gift of everlasting life. This joyous season is for sharing the love that was first shared by God two thousand years ago in the little town of Bethlehem.

People have always loved to tell stories about their favorite traditions and customs. As unique ideas and symbols became associated with Christmas, imaginative people created stories to explain their origins.

THE LEGEND OF THE CHRISTMAS ROSE

Little Madelon was a shepherd girl tending her father's lambs on a hillside near Bethlehem. As she watched the animals, she saw a group of shepherds hurrying past. Madelon asked them where they were going, and they told her of the holy child born that night. They were taking gifts of fruit, honey, and a snow white dove to the baby.

The shepherds went on, but Madelon stayed behind. She, too, wanted to see the infant Christ, but she had nothing to give him. When the poor shepherdess knelt weeping in the snow, an angel saw her. As the angel touched each fallen tear, a beautiful, pale pink rose appeared in its place.

Joy replaced Madelon's sadness, and she quickly gathered the delicate blossoms. Then she ran all the way to Bethlehem. There she presented the beautiful bouquet to Mary as a gift for her newborn son. Since that time, the Christmas rose blooms each year in December to remind the world of the simple gift of love given by a shepherd girl.

THE LEGEND OF THE CHRISTMAS SPIDER

Once there was a poor widow who lived with her children in a tiny cottage. Although she did not have money to buy them many gifts, she was determined to decorate a Christmas tree. She cut a tree in the forest, and, after the children were in bed on Christmas Eve, she decorated it with a few pieces of fruit, nuts, and some cookies she had baked. Then she fell into bed, exhausted, and worried that her little ones would have a poor Christmas.

There were spiders living in the nooks and corners of the little cottage, and they had watched the widow's work. While she slept, the spiders crept from their hiding places and climbed all over the Christmas tree, leaving silken webs as they went from branch to branch. The Christ child saw both the widow's sadness and the spiders' webs, and he turned the fragile strands to silver.

When the widow and her children awoke on Christmas morning, they were amazed to see the beautiful tree sparkling in the sun. From that day on, people have hung strands of silver tinsel on their Christmas trees, and many families place a tiny glass or golden spider on one of the boughs to recall this miracle.